D0821914

Ganeri, Anita, 1961-
Red kangaroo /

c2011.
33305223746706
sa   11/14/11

A Day in the Life: Desert Animals

Red Kangaroo

Anita Ganeri

Heinemann
LIBRARY
Chicago, Illinois

www.heinemannraintree.com
Visit our website to find out
more information about
Heinemann-Raintree books.

To order:
☎ Phone 888-454-2279
🖳 Visit www.heinemannraintree.com
to browse our catalog and order online.

© 2011 Heinemann Library
an imprint of Capstone Global Library, LLC
Chicago, Illinois

All rights reserved. No part of this publication may be
reproduced or transmitted in any form or by any means,
electronic or mechanical, including photocopying,
recording, taping, or any information storage and retrieval
system, without permission in writing from the publisher.

Edited by Daniel Nunn, Rebecca Rissman, and Sian Smith
Designed by Richard Parker
Picture research by Elizabeth Alexander
Production by Victoria Fitzgerald
Originated by Capstone Global Library Ltd
Printed and bound in China by South China Printing
 Company Ltd

14 13 12 11 10
10 9 8 7 6 5 4 3 2 1

**Library of Congress Cataloging-in-
Publication Data**
Ganeri, Anita, 1961–
  Red kangaroo / Anita Ganeri.
    p. cm. — (A day in the life. Desert animals)
  Includes bibliographical references and index.
  ISBN 978-1-4329-4774-3 (hc)
  ISBN 978-1-4329-4783-5 (pb)
1. Red kangaroo—Juvenile literature. I. Title.
  QL737.M35G36 2011
  599.2'223—dc22   2010022822

Acknowledgments
The author and publisher are grateful to the following
for permission to reproduce copyright material: Alamy
pp. 11 (© Arco Images GmbH), 15 (© Juniors Bildarchiv),
19, 23 glossary mammal (© Avico Ltd), 20 (© David
Hosking); Corbis pp. 5, 23 marsupial, 23 glossary pouch
(© Frank Krahmer), 8 (© Martin Harvey), 13, 14, (© Frans
Lanting); FLPA p. 21 (Tom and Pam Gardner); Photolibrary
pp. 7, 23 glossary desert (Image Source), 9 (Corbis),
10, 22 (Konrad Wothe/OSF), 12, 23 glossary graze
(Jim Tuten/OSF), 16, 23 glossary mob (Gerard Lacz/
Peter Arnold Images), 17, 23 glossary dingo, 23 glossary
predator (Jurgen + Christine Sohns/Picture Press), 18
(Root Alan and Joan/OSF); Shutterstock p. 4 (© Rafael
Ramirez Lee).

Front cover photograph of a red kangaroo (Macropus
rufus) in Finke Gorge National Park, Australia, reproduced
with permission of FLPA (© Frans Lanting).

Back cover photograph of (left) a kangaroo's pouch
reproduced with permission of Corbis (© Frank Krahmer);
and (right) a red kangaroo in the Australian Outback,
reproduced with permission of Photolibrary (Corbis).

We would like to thank Michael Bright for his assistance in
the preparation of this book.

Every effort has been made to contact copyright holders
of material reproduced in this book. Any omissions will
be rectified in subsequent printings if notice is given to
the publisher.

All the Internet addresses (URLs) given in this book were
valid at the time of going to press. However, due to the
dynamic nature of the Internet, some addresses may have
changed, or sites may have changed or ceased to exist
since publication. While the author and publisher regret
any inconvenience this may cause readers, no responsibility
for any such changes can be accepted by either the author
or the publisher.

Contents

Some words are shown in bold, **like this**.
You can find them in the glossary on page 23.

What Is a Red Kangaroo?

A red kangaroo is a **mammal**.

All mammals have some hair on their bodies and feed their babies milk.

pouch

Red kangaroos belong to a group of mammals called **marsupials**.

A female marsupial has a **pouch** on her body where her baby feeds and grows.

Where Do Red Kangaroos Live?

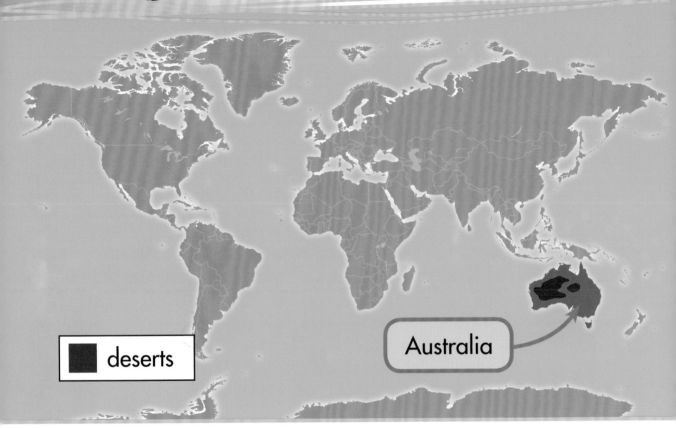

deserts

Australia

Red kangaroos live in the **deserts** of Australia.

Can you find these deserts on the map?

It is hot and dry in the desert.

The ground is mostly rocky and sandy, and there are only a few trees for shade.

What Do Red Kangaroos Look Like?

female

male

Red kangaroos are big and strong, with short, red-brown fur.

Males are larger than females. They stand taller than an adult human.

front leg

back leg

Kangaroos have huge back legs and feet for hopping.

Their front legs are much shorter.

What Do Red Kangaroos Do in the Evening?

During the day, it is very hot in the **desert**.

Red kangaroos start looking for food in the evening, when it is cooler.

A red kangaroo may **graze** all night long if there is plenty of food.

Its eyes are very good at seeing in the dark.

What Do Red Kangaroos Eat?

Red kangaroos **graze** on grass and other **desert** plants.

They sit on their back legs and lean down to feed.

There is not much water in the desert, but red kangaroos can go for a long time without drinking.

They get water from the plants they eat.

How Do Red Kangaroos Move?

At night, red kangaroos travel long distances to find food.

They move by hopping on their huge back legs.

A red kangaroo hops along in giant leaps.

It uses its long tail to help it balance as it hops along.

Do Red Kangaroos Live in Groups?

Red kangaroos usually live in small groups of up to 10 animals.

A group of kangaroos is called a **mob**.

dingo

While the kangaroos eat, they listen closely for **dingoes** and other **predators**.

The kangaroos thump the ground with their feet to warn the others of danger.

What Do Baby Red Kangaroos Look Like?

joey

A newborn red kangaroo, or joey, is only about the size of a bee.

It crawls into its mother's **pouch**, where it drinks milk and grows.

When the joey is about seven months old, it comes out of the pouch for the first time.

But it hops back in if it is frightened.

What Do Red Kangaroos Do During the Day?

In the morning, red kangaroos
stop **grazing**.

They find a shady tree where they
can spend the day resting or sleeping.

If a red kangaroo gets too hot, it sometimes licks its front legs to cool down.

In the evening, it starts grazing again.

Red Kangaroo Body Map

ear

nose

eye

mouth

fur

front leg

claws

tail

back leg

foot

Glossary

 **desert** very dry place that is rocky, stony, or sandy

 **dingo** type of wild dog that lives in Australia

 **graze** feed on grass and plants

 **mammal** animal that feeds its babies milk. All mammals have some hair or fur on their bodies.

 **marsupial** mammal with a pouch on its body

 **mob** group of kangaroos

 **pouch** like a big pocket

 **predator** animal that hunts other animals for food

Find Out More

Books

Haldane, Elizabeth. *Desert: Around the Clock with the Animals of the Desert* (24 Hours). New York: Dorling Kindersley, 2006.

Hodge, Deborah. *Desert Animals* (Who Lives Here?). Toronto: Kids Can Press, 2008.

MacAulay, Kelley, and Bobbie Kalman. *Desert Habitat* (Introducing Habitats). New York: Crabtree, 2008.

Websites

Learn more about red kangaroos at: **http://animals.nationalgeographic. com/animals/mammals/red-kangaroo/**

Learn more facts at: **www.sandiegozoo.org/animalbytes/t-kangaroo.html**

Index